Original title:
Icy Reflections

Copyright © 2024 Swan Charm
All rights reserved.

Author: Linda Leevike
ISBN HARDBACK: 978-9916-79-597-2
ISBN PAPERBACK: 978-9916-79-598-9
ISBN EBOOK: 978-9916-79-599-6

**Clarity in the Cold**

Breath of winter fills the air,
Frosty whispers everywhere.
Crystal shards on branches gleam,
Nature settles in a dream.

Silent hills adorned in white,
Stars like diamonds shining bright.
Footsteps crunch on snow's soft bed,
In the stillness, thoughts are fed.

Morning light breaks through the haze,
Painting shadows with its rays.
Clarity in every sight,
Wraps the world in pure delight.

## Nature's Shivering Canvas

Bare trees sway in the cold breeze,
Whispers of the chill tease.
Underneath the frosted sky,
Color fades and yet we sigh.

Fields of white and muted grey,
Nature's art on full display.
Each breath rises like a cloud,
Softly wrapped, we stand unbowed.

Winter paints in shades so bright,
Embracing dark with purest light.
With each gust, the canvas shifts,
A breathtaking world of winter gifts.

## **Crisp Moments**

Morning dew on blades of grass,
Whispers of the past do pass.
A lone bird sings a sweet refrain,
Echoes float through cool, clear rain.

Every breath in the chilly air,
Reminds us of the beauty rare.
Fleeting seconds, sharp and bright,
Moments captured in fading light.

With laughter shared on frosty days,
We weave our lives in lovely ways.
Crisp moments like the falling snow,
In our hearts, forever glow.

**Glistening Echoes**

Snowflakes dance on silent nights,
Reflecting all the starry lights.
Each flake tells a story clear,
Whispers carried through the year.

Nature's breath in silver hues,
Chill invites the world to muse.
Glistening echoes in the dark,
Softly speaking, leaving marks.

Footprints lead through winter's dream,
Sparkling like a diamond seam.
Every sound, a gentle sigh,
In this world, we learn to fly.

## **Glimmering Surfaces**

Reflecting light on the lake,
Smooth as glass in the dawn,
Whispers of dreams awake,
The day bids night farewell.

Ripples dance in the breeze,
Nature's pulse slows down,
Captured moments of ease,
A harmony of sound.

Shadows stretch and sway,
Beneath the willow's grace,
Each hour fades away,
Time slows its swift race.

Colors blend and play,
In a canvas of blue,
As twilight steals the day,
The stars begin to view.

Glimmers fade into night,
A soft, enchanting scene,
In silence, they unite,
Where dreams are evergreen.

**Ice-Cast Garlands**

Hanging from boughs with care,
Sparkling chains of frost,
In the chilling winter air,
Beauty at nature's cost.

Crystals gleam, softly bright,
Adorning every tree,
A delicate, frozen sight,
In a silent reverie.

Whispers of a frozen breeze,
Carrying secrets untold,
Amongst the whispered trees,
The air, crisp and bold.

Nature's artistry unfolds,
In the glow of pale light,
Icicles like stories told,
Suspended in the night.

Awaiting the thawing sun,
They shimmer, they will fade,
But for now, they hold on,
To the magic they've made.

## Fragments of the Frozen Mind

In a stillness of thought,
Memories, sharp and clear,
Echoes of battles fought,
In the chill, they appear.

Shattered dreams on the ground,
Pieces of what was known,
Lost whispers all around,
A heart that's turned to stone.

Fractured reflections glow,
In the depths of despair,
Haunting shadows throw,
Ghosts that linger there.

Yet from the frost, a spark,
Of hope begins to bloom,
Lighting up the dark,
Dispelling every gloom.

In the quiet of the mind,
A warmth begins to flow,
To mend what's left behind,
And let the lost things grow.

## Shivers of Starlight

In the velvet night sky,
Stars shimmer, bright and bold,
Winking as time slips by,
Secrets of ages old.

Each twinkle tells a tale,
Of worlds that spin and weave,
In silence, they unveil,
The wonder we believe.

Glimmers wrap the dark,
With a tender embrace,
As dreams take flight and spark,
In this vast, endless space.

Echoes of distant light,
Travel through time and air,
Guiding hearts with their flight,
In a dance of silent prayer.

Starlight's shivers cascade,
Over mountains and seas,
In this night serenade,
Infinite mysteries.

## Reflections in a Shard of Ice

Beneath the pale blue skies,
I find a fragile peace,
In every crystal gaze,
A moment's sweet release.

Time whispers through the glint,
Memories held so tight,
Each shard a silent truth,
In the shimmering light.

Echoes of the past,
Dance in winter's chill,
Reflections of my heart,
Frozen yet so still.

The world, a canvas pure,
Painted with the cold,
In every little spark,
A story to be told.

Amid these icy dreams,
I chase the whispered sighs,
In every fleeting glimpse,
I find where beauty lies.

## **Embrace of the Frost**

The morning sun breaks through,
With fingers cold and bright,
Caressing every branch,
In a soft, tender light.


Crisp air within my lungs,
A sweet and biting kiss,
Nature's gentle touch,
Wraps me in its bliss.


Footprints mark the path,
Leading through the white,
Each step a quiet song,
In pure, sparkling light.


Beneath the frosted trees,
I pause and turn around,
The world a silken dream,
In crystalline surround.


With every breeze that blows,
I feel the winter's grace,
An embrace of the frost,
In this enchanted space.

## Translucent Tears

When winter nights reveal,
The secrets of the stars,
Tears of ice cascade down,
From the heavens afar.

Each droplet tells a tale,
Of longing and of loss,
Translucent, delicate,
Reflecting every cross.

A symphony of sighs,
In the hush of the night,
Gathering like whispers,
In the soft, silver light.

Underneath the velvet sky,
These tears begin to meld,
With hopes and dreams long gone,
In silence, they are held.

Yet in their fragile form,
There's beauty so profound,
Translucent as they fall,
In their grace, I'm found.

**Breath of the Snowbound**

In the hush of falling snow,
A stillness wraps the land,
Each flake a whispered breath,
Caressing nature's hand.


The world is soft and white,
A blanket thick and warm,
Embracing all that sleeps,
Within the winter's charm.


Footsteps softly linger,
On pathways made of dreams,
As echoes of the past,
Float on silver streams.


With every frost-kissed morn,
A new tale starts to weave,
In the breath of snowbound,
There's wonder to believe.


Let the heart rejoice,
In this serene delight,
For in the snow's embrace,
We find our purest light.

# **Frosted Memories**

In the hush of winter's breath,
Footprints fade beneath the snow,
Echoes of laughter linger,
Time dances softly, moving slow.

Shadows play on frozen lakes,
Branches draped in white embrace,
Whispers warm the chilling air,
Memories time cannot erase.

The sparkle of a twilight glow,
Pictures held between our hearts,
Each moment like a crystal,
In a world where love imparts.

We trace the lines of what was lost,
Holding on to fleeting dreams,
Like frost upon the windowpanes,
In the silence, nothing seems.

Yet still the warmth of stories shared,
Melts the ice of solitude,
Within these frosted memories,
Hope awakens, life renewed.

## **Crystal Clear Contemplations**

In quiet moments, thoughts arise,
Like bubbles in a crystal stream,
Reflections clear upon the surface,
Woven deep in quiet dream.

Each thought an orb of glistening light,
Floating softly in the air,
Carried by the whispered winds,
Guided by a knowing prayer.

Questions dance like spinning leaves,
Fall and rise with gentle grace,
Searching depths of inner peace,
In the heart, a sacred place.

The world beyond, a fleeting blur,
In silence, clarity is found,
Every breath a deepening sigh,
In contemplation, we are bound.

With every thought, like raindrops fall,
A symphony of tranquil sound,
In the stillness of the night,
Crystal clear, the truth unbound.

## Glistening Secrets

In the twilight's gentle glow,
Secrets sparkle, soft and bright,
Hidden truths beneath the stars,
Whispered softly, out of sight.

Each moment holds a quiet tale,
Wrapped in silver, spun from dreams,
Thoughts entwined, like vines that grow,
In the night, their magic gleams.

The moonbeams dance on water's face,
Breathless sighs of stories shared,
Hearts entwined in mystery,
In the hush, we know we dared.

Underneath the tangled branches,
Glistening secrets, softly spoken,
In the twilight, love revives,
In silence, bonds are never broken.

With every glance, a universe,
Stories shared, both old and new,
Glistening under starry skies,
In the night, our hearts are true.

## **Shivers of Reflection**

As autumn leaves begin to fall,
Shivers race through time and space,
Echoes of a brisk embrace,
Leave reminders of their call.

In the stillness, shadows twist,
Each whisper holds a haunted grace,
Reflections dance on surfaces,
A haunting song, a misty tryst.

Glimmers of the past arise,
In the twilight's softening glow,
Rising like the morning mist,
Giving way to what we know.

Through the corridors of thought,
Shivers of our histories play,
Piecing memories like a quilt,
Each stitch a moment of the day.

Yet in the cold, a fire burns,
Warmth of love against the frost,
Through reflection, we can find,
That no moment is ever lost.

## **Shard of Frosted Light**

In winter's gentle embrace, cold and bright,
Glimmers dance in the soft pale light.
Each fragment holds a fleeting glow,
A world aglow with dreams below.

Whispers swirl on a frosty breeze,
Nature's secrets hide between the trees.
A sigh of silence fills the air,
While shadows weave their crystal snare.

A moment caught, pure and rare,
Time suspended in the frosty glare.
Reflecting all that yet may be,
A shard of light, a memory.

Deep within the frozen maze,
A shimmer fades, revealing ways.
Through paths unknown, we dare to seek,
In shards of light, we find our peak.

The night descends, and stars take flight,
Embracing dreams that feel so right.
In every fragment, hope ignites,
A shard of frost, a guide in nights.

## Icebound Visions

Beneath the frost, the visions lie,
Dreams encased, where echoes die.
Reflections shimmer on the glass,
As time flows slow, like melting glass.

Each breath a cloud in chilly air,
A silent wish, a whispered prayer.
In frozen realms, where shadows dwell,
The heart reveals its silent spell.

Through icy veins, the stories sprawl,
Brittle truths that softly call.
A gentle touch, a fleeting glance,
In icebound dreams, we take our chance.

Awakened by the morning sun,
The visions fade, the race begun.
Yet in each drop that melts away,
A trace of hope, a bright bouquet.

As seasons shift and stories tell,
In icebound moments, we find our well.
To rise anew, to break the mold,
In visions bright, our dreams unfold.

## **Midnight in a Glass Cathedral**

Underneath the velvet sky,
A glass cathedral reaches high.
Stars alight in silken threads,
As midnight whispers softly spreads.

Through crystalline arches, shadows glide,
Echoes linger, secrets hide.
With every breath, the stillness sings,
A serenade of hidden things.

The moon spills light on icy floors,
Each glimmer opens unseen doors.
In this place of dreams confined,
The heart and soul intertwine.

Cloaked in shades of cobalt blue,
The glass reflects a world anew.
In each visage, stories pause,
A midnight dance without a cause.

Outside, the world is lost in sleep,
Yet within, the memories seep.
In this cathedral made of light,
Midnight glows, eternally bright.

## Crystal Clear Sorrows

Each tear, a crystal, pure and bright,
Caught in time's relentless flight.
In every drop, a tale unfolds,
Of love, of loss, of dreams untold.

The wind carries whispers soft and low,
Secrets buried deep in the snow.
As memories fade like morning mist,
The heart aches for what was missed.

Through crystal shards where shadows play,
The light reveals the price we pay.
Reflections weave a story grand,
Of fragile hope, of weathered land.

In silent nights, our sorrows dance,
A fleeting glimpse, a second chance.
So we embrace the pain we keep,
In crystal clear, our souls do weep.

Yet in each tear, a lesson's born,
Through sorrow's veil, we are reborn.
In crystal clear, we find our way,
Through darkest nights, to brighter days.

## Veils of Winter

Snowflakes dance in gentle flight,
Whispers weave through silent night.
Trees wear cloaks of sparkling white,
Nature's breath, a frosty sight.

Firelight flickers, shadows sway,
Warmth and stillness softly play.
Wrapped in layers, we find peace,
In this cold, let worries cease.

Footprints mark the snowy ground,
In this hush, a magic found.
Stars above, a distant glow,
Guiding paths where dreams can flow.

Every breath a crystal sigh,
Winter's lullabies drift by.
In the still, hearts softly ponder,
Time stands still, we drift and wander.

As dawn breaks with rosy light,
Veils of winter, pure and bright.
In the frost, our spirits gleam,
Wrapped in warmth, we dare to dream.

## **Dreaming in Chill**

Dreams unfurl in frosty air,
Whispers cradle every care.
Underneath the silvery moon,
Hearts are swaying to night's tune.

Moonlit snow on fields so wide,
Hidden dreams we cannot bide.
With every chill, a story waits,
In the night, the heart relates.

Eyes closed tight, we drift away,
Into realms where shadows play.
In the silence, secrets breathe,
Wrapped in warmth, our souls believe.

Frosty windows lace with art,
In the chill, we find our start.
Each breath forms a fleeting cloud,
In our dreams, we feel so proud.

As dawn tiptoes, dreams may fade,
Yet the chill will never jade.
In the quiet, we take flight,
Dreaming softly in the night.

## **Shadows of the Deep Freeze**

In the depths where shadows creep,
Winter holds her secrets deep.
Frosty tendrils, cold embrace,
Whispers echo in this space.

Trees stand tall in silver veils,
Carried on the wind's soft gales.
In their boughs, the silence clings,
Every branch and creature sings.

Frozen lakes reflect the sky,
Beneath the ice, the stillness lie.
In this realm of pale and gray,
Life sleeps tight till spring's ballet.

Footsteps crunch on icy ground,
In this hush, a world profound.
Nature's breath held tight in freeze,
Captured moments, fleeting ease.

As dusk falls with a velvet sigh,
Stars awaken, twinkling high.
In the shadows, dreams ignite,
In the deep freeze, pure delight.

## **Icebound Thoughts**

Thoughts like snowflakes softly drift,
In the ice, our visions lift.
Frigid breezes, tales untold,
In quiet moments, dreams unfold.

Each reflection, crystal clear,
In the stillness, we draw near.
Wonder weaves through frosty air,
Chasing echoes everywhere.

Chilled sensations take their form,
Carving pathways, hearts grow warm.
In this space, our spirits rise,
Underneath the winter skies.

Lurking deep in frozen still,
Thoughts awaken, time to fill.
As the frost bites at our cheeks,
Within the cold, our passion speaks.

In this world of gleaming light,
Icebound thoughts take glorious flight.
Embracing all that winter brings,
In the chill, our spirit sings.

## Sparkling Dilemmas

In the twilight dance of light,
Choices glimmer, sparkling bright.
Each decision, a fleeting flame,
Caught in whispers, none the same.

Paths diverge beneath the stars,
Leading hearts to distant jars.
With each step, the shadows play,
As night devours the light of day.

A gleam of hope, a hint of doubt,
In silence, feelings twist about.
Dreams collide, like waves at sea,
A shimmering glimpse of what could be.

The heart weighs heavy, yet it flies,
Amidst the sparkles in the skies.
Each dilemma wrapped in gold,
An adventure waiting to unfold.

With courage found in glistening tears,
We chase the light beyond our fears.
In every choice, a story spun,
In sparkling dilemmas, we are one.

## **Frosted Realities**

In the hush of winter's breath,
Reality dons a cloak of death.
Frosted tales on window panes,
Whispered truths, forgotten names.

Beneath the chill, the world stands still,
A quiet war of heart and will.
Dreams like smoke in bitter air,
Fragile hopes, a silent prayer.

The sun's embrace, a distant wish,
In icy streams, our thoughts disperse.
We tread on paths of shimmering white,
Seeking warmth in fading light.

With every step, the echoes freeze,
Moments gone, like autumn leaves.
Yet in the cold, we find our grace,
In frosted realities, we find our place.

Each heartbeat soft, like whispered sighs,
Reflections dance in frosty skies.
Though the chill may numb our souls,
In the frost, a beauty unfolds.

## Cold Gemstones

In vaults of ice, the treasures lie,
Cold gemstones glint, a muted cry.
Shards of dreams, encased in blue,
Fleeting moments, pure and true.

Each gem a tale, a fractured light,
Caught in shadows of the night.
With every cut, a story told,
Of hearts entwined, yet hearts so cold.

Amongst the gleams of frozen fire,
Desires dance, ignite the desire.
Yet, lost in chilling solitude,
The spark remains, in cold imbued.

A treasure sought in icy grasp,
Gemstones glisten, hope we clasp.
In silence lies their fragile song,
A symphony where we belong.

Though cold the world, we search the night,
For warmth in stones that catch the light.
Each facet holds our whispered dreams,
Cold gemstones reflect our schemes.

## Frigid Echoes

In the stillness of the night,
Frigid echoes take their flight.
Voices whisper through the trees,
Carried softly on the breeze.

Beneath the stars, a haunting call,
Resonates in shadows tall.
Through the dark, they weave and sway,
Reminders of the closing day.

Memory dances on the frost,
In frigid winds, what's gained, what's lost?
Each echo holds a tale once warm,
Now encased in winter's charm.

As silence falls, we dare to hear,
The frigid echoes drawing near.
In every sound, a thread of soul,
Binding together, making whole.

With every chill, a spark ignites,
Frigid echoes tell their sights.
In the cold, we find our voice,
In whispered echoes, we rejoice.

## Glacial Whispers

Beneath the frost, a secret sigh,
The mountains echo, low and high.
Amidst the chill, a soft refrain,
Nature's voice, in crystal chain.

In shadows deep, the cold winds speak,
Of ancient tales, of strength and meek.
Each flake a note, each gust a sound,
In winter's hold, where dreams abound.

The glaciers move, a slow ballet,
A timeless dance, both night and day.
Their whispers carry through the breeze,
A melody that stirs the freeze.

In silence thick, a world aglow,
With icy breath, the valleys know.
The stillness sings, a haunting tune,
A lullaby beneath the moon.

As twilight fades, the stars ignite,
In glacial realms, a spark of light.
Each shimmer holds eternity,
A secret kept by land and sea.

## **Frigid Images**

A canvas white, pure and untouched,
The world lies still, with beauty clutched.
Frosted branches, like works of art,
Nature's brush, a frozen heart.

Reflections dance on icy lakes,
In crystal forms, the silence wakes.
With every glance, a story weaves,
In winter's grip, the magic breathes.

Snowflakes fall, a gentle line,
Each one a gem, a spark divine.
They quilt the earth in soft embrace,
A quiet hush, a peaceful space.

Through frosted air, the chill prevails,
The wind's soft touch, through whispered trails.
Each scene a dream, a fleeting light,
In frigid realms, where day meets night.

In frozen time, with clarity,
We sketch the world, with reverie.
With every breath, the cold ignites,
The heart of winter, pure delights.

## **Frozen Reverberations**

The echoes of a winter's night,
Resound in silence, soft and bright.
Each frozen note, a sound profound,
In frost's embrace, the air is crowned.

A distant chime of glacial bells,
Ring through valleys, where quiet dwells.
With every pulse, the cold expands,
In whispered tones, time softly stands.

The icebound rivers weave and flow,
In rhythmic beats, through highs and lows.
Polar winds, like songs, they sing,
The harmony of winter's cling.

Reflections dart on surfaces clear,
As if the stars themselves drew near.
In twilight's glow, the shadows play,
Eternal dance, in frosty spray.

With each heartbeat, the world aligns,
In frozen realms, where time unwinds.
Reverberations fill the skies,
In winter's song, the spirit flies.

## Shimmering Solitude

Alone beneath the starry shroud,
In frosted air, I stand unbowed.
The night embraces, soft and true,
A shimmering glow, a world anew.

Each breath I take, the silence sings,
In solitude, my spirit flings.
The snowflakes twirl, a dance of light,
In quiet grace, they take their flight.

Amongst the trees, a tranquil peace,
Where frozen whispers cease to cease.
The beauty hushes all despair,
In solitude, I find my prayer.

A glimmering path, the stars await,
A journey through the night, sedate.
With every step, the world ignites,
In shimmering calm, my heart ignites.

With nature's breath, I intertwine,
In solitude, the stars align.
A cosmic dance, forever spun,
In shimmering stillness, I am one.

## The Language of Winter's Edge

Whispers drift on frosty air,
Words of silence everywhere,
Nature speaks in muted tones,
Crystals gleam on barren bones.

Branches heavy, laden down,
Nature's hush, a velvet crown,
Shadows stretch beneath the trees,
Winter's breath, a haunting breeze.

Footprints mark the icy ground,
Echoes of a world profound,
Frigid beauty, stark and clear,
In the stillness, we draw near.

The heart of winter softly glows,
In its grasp, a warmth that grows,
Embrace the chill, let it teach,
Messages the frost can preach.

Underneath the silver skies,
Hope emerges, never dies,
In each flake, a tale to tell,
In winter's edge, we know it well.

## Glimpses Through the Frost

Windows painted white with grace,
Hidden worlds behind their face,
Frosted patterns, lace-like art,
Nature's touch, a secret start.

Tiny creatures wait, abide,
Through the chill, they bide their time,
Glimpses fleeting, winter's trance,
Nature's rhythm, quiet dance.

Ice and snow in gentle sway,
Marking time, each fleeting day,
Sunrise casts a golden hue,
Breaking through, a world anew.

Shapes of shadow, forms of light,
In this realm, we find delight,
Every breath a frosty plume,
In cold's embrace, feel the bloom.

Through the glass, we stand and stare,
Winter's wonder everywhere,
Each moment held in crisp embrace,
A fleeting glimpse, a sacred space.

## Elysium of the Cold

In the hush of frosty morn,
Whispers of a world reborn,
Shimmering in silver light,
Beauty rests, a pure delight.

Snowflakes dance on gentle breeze,
Nature's laughter through the trees,
Every flake, a story spun,
In the cold, we are all one.

Mountains clad in powdered white,
Radiate in morning's bright,
Echoes call from far and wide,
In this frozen realm, abide.

Hearts entwined in winter's chill,
Finding warmth in quiet thrill,
In the Elysium we roam,
A shimmering path, we find home.

Beneath the stars, they softly gleam,
In the night, we weave a dream,
Elysium of cold and grace,
In this moment, we embrace.

## Dance of the Shimmering Surface

Underneath the moonlit glow,
Ice reflects a world below,
Shimmering with whispers sweet,
Echoes of our hearts' soft beat.

Nature sways in crystal bands,
Winter waltzes, takes our hands,
Each ripple, every glide,
In this dance, we take the ride.

Footfalls crack on frozen sea,
In this moment, wild and free,
Skaters twirl in gleeful joy,
Childlike laughter, purest ploy.

Frigid breeze that bites and stings,
Yet in our hearts, the warmth it brings,
Stories woven through the ice,
In this dance, we find our dice.

As the stars begin to fade,
In the twilight, dreams are made,
Dance of ice, a fleeting bliss,
In winter's song, we find our kiss.

## **Below the Surface Glaze**

Beneath the icy sheen we walk,
A world encased in frozen talk.
Reflections dance in silver light,
Whispers echo through the night.

Hidden depths that lie so deep,
Secrets that the shadows keep.
Silent stories tangled tight,
In the shimmer, lost from sight.

Footprints trace the quiet ground,
In this realm, no dreams are found.
A mirror image of the soul,
Time stands still, the heart feels whole.

The frost-kissed air wraps around,
Every breath, a crystal sound.
In the chill, we find our place,
A moment held in soft embrace.

So we wander, hand in hand,
Through the glimmering, silent land.
Below the ice, a pulse remains,
Life is woven through the chains.

## **Chilled Reveries**

In twilight's grip, the world holds breath,
A stillness speaks of life and death.
The night unfolds with whispered dreams,
As moonlight dances on quiet streams.

Chilled reveries in shadows grow,
Where time drifts like the falling snow.
Each flake a thought that takes its flight,
In the silence, the heart takes light.

Beneath the stars, so cold, so bright,
We chase the echoes of the night.
Fragrant air, spun in the dark,
Fires of longing spark the heart.

A journey woven through the ice,
We find our warmth in each slice.
Frosted windows, dreams unfurl,
Inside our minds, a hidden world.

Together here, we find our lane,
In the chilly, tender rain.
Chilled reveries, a sweet escape,
Wrap us in this soft landscape.

## **Frostbite Memories**

Frostbite memories pierce the air,
Each breath a ghost, a distant care.
Time is etched in crystal glaze,
A fleeting glimpse of winter's phase.

In the stillness, echoes ring,
Of laughter lost, a whispered sting.
Fragments of a bygone day,
Swirling like the snowflakes' play.

Every flake a tale untold,
Moments shimmering, bright but cold.
Through crystal branches, shadows slide,
Echoes of the past abide.

Frostbite's kiss upon the skin,
Recalls the warmth that once had been.
Softly, the world turns to gray,
Yet memories will never sway.

With every chill, a story breathes,
In winter's grasp, a heart believes.
Frostbite memories, a gentle shroud,
In silence wrapped, beneath the cloud.

## The Stillness of the Glade

In a glade where shadows linger long,
The world feels muted, soft, and strong.
Among the trees, the silence reigns,
Whispers of nature, lost in chains.

The stillness wraps like a velvet cloak,
Each gentle sigh, a quiet stroke.
Sunbeams filter through the leaves,
In this peace, the heart believes.

Echoes fade in the dusky air,
Time stands still, a moment rare.
Here, the soul can find its grace,
As nature paints a tranquil space.

Mossy beds invite a pause,
While nature sings without a cause.
Underfoot, the soft ground breathes,
In the stillness, the spirit weaves.

With every rustle, life unfolds,
In muted hues and stories told.
The stillness of the glade still calls,
Where the heart remembers, and the quiet falls.

## **Frost-Kissed Thoughts**

In the silence of dawn's breath,
Thoughts awaken like soft snow,
Whispers of winter's quiet charm,
Wrapped in a cool, tender glow.

Glistening dreams on frosted panes,
Each flicker tells a tale untold,
Wandering through this crystal haze,
Where memories shimmer, bright and bold.

A chill runs deep within the air,
Embracing all that it might claim,
Frosted leaves in gentle prayer,
Whispering softly each sweet name.

In this moment, time stands still,
As frosted thoughts gracefully dance,
Echoes of peace, a soothing thrill,
Lost in the winter's chilly trance.

So let the frost-kissed world unfold,
From branches bare to skies so grey,
In quiet grace, a beauty old,
A wintry peace that will not sway.

## Ethereal Glaciers

Beneath the moon's enchanting light,
Glaciers glow with a sacred hue,
Carving paths both grand and slight,
Nature's canvas, pure and true.

Fragmented shards of ice reflect,
Stories woven through the night,
Whispers echo, hearts connect,
In the stillness, pure delight.

Frozen rivers, crystal trails,
Carry secrets of the land,
Where each flake of ice unveils,
A world crafted by nature's hand.

Ethereal beauty, cold and rare,
Glistening under starlit skies,
A moment caught, suspended air,
In a dance where silence lies.

Beneath the weight of winter's breath,
Glaciers cradle time's great flow,
In their presence, a sense of depth,
Eternal truths carved in snow.

## Clear as Ice

In the chill of a winter's morn,
Crystal clarity arrives,
Nature's jewels, delicately worn,
In silence, the world thrives.

Each breath a fog, a gentle sigh,
Frosty fingers touch the ground,
Underneath the vast blue sky,
Hidden wonders can be found.

Glossy surfaces glide with grace,
Reflecting dreams and hopes anew,
Every glimpse a tender trace,
Of the pure, the bright, the true.

With every step on icy trails,
The heart beats in steady time,
As winter whispers, softly hails,
A beauty wrapped in gentle rhyme.

Clear as ice, the spirit beams,
Embracing all that life imparts,
In every shimmer, hope redeems,
A winter's tale that stirs the heart.

## Chilling Reflections

Upon the lake, the silence drapes,
Mirrors of twilight's vibrant hue,
Chilling reflections, nature shapes,
In stillness, old becomes anew.

Branches bare, like fingers stretch,
Scratching skies both wide and grey,
In this canvas, hearts will etch,
The dreams that dance and fade away.

Icicles hang like wishes cast,
Dripping slowly from time's embrace,
Each moment cherished, held steadfast,
In the chill, we find our place.

A haunting beauty wrapped in frost,
Calls to the spirit, pure and bright,
In the echoes, we gain and lost,
Chilling reflections of the night.

So let us wander, hand in hand,
Through this frosty, dreamlike glow,
In reflections, we'll understand,
The magic that the cold can show.

## **Shattered Glimmers**

In shards of light they dance and play,
Fragments of dreams, they fade away.
A whisper of hope in the twilight's glow,
Lost in the echoes of what we know.

Through cracks in the glass, the sunbeam spills,
Bringing warmth to the heart, igniting thrills.
Yet shadows linger, a haunting trace,
Of broken moments we can't replace.

The mirror reflects a fractured past,
Yet in the pieces, beauty's cast.
Each glimmer shines with stories untold,
In the remains, pure hearts unfold.

Time weaves the shards with delicate grace,
Turning the pain into a warm embrace.
As glimmers twinkle in the darkened night,
We find our strength in the shattered light.

So here we stand, with hope alight,
Embracing the broken, the lost, the fight.
For in every fissure, a lesson lies,
Shattered glimmers reflect the skies.

## Winter's Shimmer

Beneath the snow, the world lies still,
A tranquil hush, a gentle chill.
Frosted branches stretch and sigh,
Glistening softly under a pale sky.

In whispered winds, secrets flow,
Carrying tales of winter's glow.
Blankets of white on the ground so deep,
Cradle the dreams that winter keeps.

Each flake that falls, a star from above,
Whirling and twirling with grace and love.
Painting the earth in shimmering white,
A canvas bright in the quiet night.

The moon casts shadows, long and lean,
In winter's embrace, the world serene.
Every twinkle and sparkle a fleeting kiss,
A moment captured in icy bliss.

So let us wander through frosty lanes,
Breathe in the chill, forget our pains.
For in winter's shimmer, we find our way,
A sparkle of magic in the light of day.

## Crystal Tides

The ocean whispers beneath the moon,
With crystal tides that ebb and swoon.
Waves caress the shore like a lover's touch,
Carrying secrets, oh so much.

In the depths below, treasures hide,
Mirrored dreams in the tranquil tide.
Reflections dance on the water's face,
As shells reveal their hidden grace.

Each surge of water, a story told,
Of time and journeys, of the bold.
The salt-kissed air, a sweet embrace,
Calls us forth to this sacred place.

With each new wave, life begins anew,
Carving the shore, as tides pursue.
In crystal waves, our spirits flow,
Connected to the depths below.

So let us wander by ocean's side,
Embracing the rhythm of the crystal tide.
For in the waves, our hearts align,
In the dance of water, pure and divine.

## Silent Frost

In the still of dawn, a blanket lies,
Silent frost beneath the skies.
Whispers linger in the icy air,
A moment captured, beyond compare.

Each blade of grass, a crystal thread,
Glistening softly, white and red.
The world transformed by winter's kiss,
In frozen silence, there's a bliss.

Footsteps crunch on this soft carpet,
Echoes of nature, a quiet sonnet.
Branches wear their coats of lace,
Framing the beauty of this space.

Frosted windows tell tales anew,
Of cozy nights and morning dew.
In the hush of winter's gentle breath,
We find the magic that conquers death.

So let us cherish this serene scene,
In silent frost, where dreams convene.
For in the quiet, life can weave,
A tapestry of peace, if we believe.

## Glacial Soliloquy

In icy whispers, truths unfold,
A solitude, where dreams are cold,
The frozen heart, it breathes too slow,
In frozen realms, thoughts start to flow.

Each crystal flake tells secret sighs,
Beneath the moon, where silence lies,
A distant echo, the mind's retreat,
In chill's embrace, old memories meet.

The barren trees in frosty hue,
Stand sentinel to skies so blue,
A winter's tale, in shades of gray,
Silent paths where souls can stray.

In glacial depths, reach far within,
To find the light, where shadows spin,
And in the quiet, hear the call,
Of frost that dances, one and all.

So ponder here, in icy grace,
The beauty found in frozen space,
A tender heart, though encased in ice,
Will thaw with time, if taken nice.

## Frost's Embrace

Morning light on fields of white,
Soft as whispers, pure delight,
A frosty breath, a gentle kiss,
Nature's canvas, a frozen bliss.

Beneath the cover, warmth resides,
In frosty arms, the spirit hides,
A fleeting moment, time stands still,
In winter's grip, all hearts will fill.

The world awash in silver gleam,
Each icy shard, a frozen dream,
Brittle edges, sparkling bright,
Frost's embrace, a wondrous sight.

A dance of air, so crisp and clean,
Whispers of life, though seldom seen,
The quietude, a gentle plea,
In frosted arms, we wander free.

Come share the cold, the stillness rare,
In winter's hold, find solace there,
For in each breath, a story lies,
Of frost's embrace and winter skies.

## **Whitewashed Whispers**

Upon the hill, a cloak of snow,
Whitewashed whispers, soft and low,
Each fluttered flake, a tale retold,
In wintry air, the stories unfold.

Silent shadows play on ground,
A world transformed, with grace profound,
Twilight dances, soft and clear,
While winter's breath slips ever near.

With every step, the crunch of peace,
In this expanse, all troubles cease,
Where muted colors blend and fade,
In whitewashed dreams, our fears are laid.

A canvas pure, a tranquil sea,
Whispers echo, wild and free,
In frosty veins, the pulse runs deep,
In gentle lull, the earth does sleep.

Come wander through this snowy trance,
In whitewashed whispers, take your chance,
To lose yourself in nature's art,
As winter wraps around the heart.

## The Cool Touch of Reflection

In stillness found, the mirror gazes,
A frozen world, in crisp phrases,
Each breath, a fog upon the glass,
Where thoughts glide like leaves in the grass.

The cool touch of ice, a fleeting thought,
Wisdom hidden, lessons taught,
In quiet pools, the soul can see,
The echoes of who we used to be.

Through frosted frames, we glimpse the past,
Each memory, a shadow cast,
Reflections dance beneath the stars,
In the cool night's breath, we heal our scars.

The world external, painted white,
Invites us softly into the night,
With every shimmer, every glow,
The cool touch whispers what we know.

So pause awhile, let silence reign,
In this moment, let go of pain,
For in reflection, truth set free,
The cool touch reveals what's meant to be.

## Buried Reflections

In the ground, secrets lie deep,
Whispers of memories, still asleep.
Shadows linger where thoughts were sown,
A tale of silence, all alone.

Digging gently with my heart's hand,
Unearthing dreams, softly they stand.
Fleeting moments, wrapped in the clay,
Buried reflections, fade away.

Light flickers through cracks of the earth,
Bringing to life what lost its worth.
Echoes of laughter, now just a sigh,
In this quiet, old spirits lie.

Finding fragments of who I was,
Remnants of love, its silent buzz.
Each soft layer holds a surprise,
Glimpses of time beneath the skies.

As the seasons turn and shift,
Shadows dance in the sunlight's gift.
Buried reflections yearn to be free,
Awakening stories, calling to me.

## Snowy Illusions

Amidst the whiteness, dreams unfold,
Silent whispers, secrets untold.
Footprints vanish in winter's breath,
Brushing softly, a dance with death.

Flakes of crystal drift and sway,
Painting visions in shades of gray.
Illusions sparkle, clear yet blurred,
In the stillness, silence is stirred.

Each flake a story, unique and bright,
Concealing wonders from morning light.
As the sun rises, warmth drifts in,
Reality breaks, where dreams begin.

Winds carry laughter, soft and white,
Impressions lingering, pure delight.
Caught in the moment, time feels slow,
In snowy illusions, hearts overflow.

When the thaw comes, will I recall,
The magic of snow, its gentle thrall?
In every shimmer, a memory lies,
Snowy illusions beneath the skies.

## **Mirror of the North**

Reflecting light from skies so wide,
The mirror holds the land's pure pride.
Mountains rise like giants tall,
In their shadows, nature's call.

Rivers flow with tales of old,
Carving mountains, brave and bold.
Underneath the shimmering sheen,
Life unfolds, vibrant and green.

Whispers roam through the pine trees,
Carried softly by the breeze.
Every glance reveals the past,
In the north, memories cast.

Stars emerge with the night's embrace,
Glistening gems in the vast space.
A mirror's truth, it shows so clear,
A bond with nature, ever near.

Through the seasons, shifting light,
A dance of shadows, day and night.
The mirror of the north reflects,
Nature's beauty, time protects.

# Reflective Coldness

In frozen realms where whispers freeze,
The air is thick with distant pleas.
Each breath a cloud, a poignant trace,
Reflective coldness fills this space.

Frosted windows, the world obscured,
Silent thoughts, both raw and pure.
Shivers linger like fleeting dreams,
Caught in the stillness, nothing seems.

The quiet hum of winter's reign,
An echoing heart wrapped in disdain.
Yet in the cold, warmth can be found,
Amidst the chill, love's soft sound.

Navigating through the snowy night,
Stars overhead, the only light.
Reflective coldness, a tender touch,
Reminds me gently, I'm loved so much.

Though icy fingers embrace the land,
Hope still flickers, a guiding hand.
In the depths of winter's hold,
Lies a promise, brave and bold.

**Frosted Echoes**

Silence whispers through the trees,
Chill of winter in the breeze.
Footprints linger on the ground,
Lost in echoes, barely found.

Stars like diamonds in the sky,
Each a wish, a fleeting sigh.
Glaze of ice on branches high,
Nature's breath, a soft goodbye.

Moonlight casts a silver gleam,
Waking dreams from quiet stream.
Every shadow softly plays,
In the dance of winter's rays.

Frosted breath upon the air,
Whispers secrets, soft and rare.
Time stands still as nights unfold,
Each moment, a tale retold.

Yet in silence, life will grow,
Beneath the frost, the seeds will sow.
Hope will rise with each new dawn,
In the echoes, life goes on.

## **Shattered Glass Beneath**

Crystals glinting on the floor,
Nature's jewels, evermore.
With each step, a story cracks,
Whispers of the past, no tracks.

Fractured light in pieces lay,
Memories of yesterday.
Each sharp edge a tale to tell,
A silent echo, a farewell.

Beneath the surface, darkness flows,
Hidden truths nobody knows.
Fragments of a world once whole,
Shattered dreams within the soul.

To walk on shards, to feel the pain,
But beauty rises, like the rain.
With every cut, a chance to heal,
In broken glass, we find what's real.

And so we tread through shards of light,
Finding hope within the night.
From shattered glass, we rise anew,
In pieces, strength to see us through.

## A Mirror of Winter's Breath

A quiet lake holds winter's gaze,
Reflecting life in frozen maze.
Frigid winds weave softest threads,
A tapestry where stillness treads.

Breath of ice upon my skin,
Whispers secrets deep within.
Time suspended, a moment's grace,
Captured softly in this place.

Branches bow with glittering crowns,
While gentle snowflakes drift down.
Nature breathes in soothing sighs,
A mirror where the spirit lies.

Echoes of a world so bright,
Cloaked in soft and purest white.
Stillness reigns in winter's hold,
In this quiet, dreams unfold.

Yet beneath the icy sheen,
Life stirs softly, calm and keen.
A mirror waits for seeds to cast,
In winter's breath, many shadows last.

## **Glacial Dreams**

In the hush of snowy night,
Dreams drift softly into sight.
Glacial whispers, cool and clear,
Carving paths for hopes sincere.

Stars like lanterns pave the way,
Guiding lost souls who stray.
Frozen rivers hold the past,
In their depths, reflections cast.

Mountains cradle silent fears,
Echoes of forgotten years.
Veils of ice on tranquil streams,
Hold the secrets of our dreams.

Windswept tales in midnight blue,
Paint the sky with dreams anew.
Each flake falling, pure and free,
Carves a future yet to be.

And in this glacial reverie,
We find beauty's clarity.
With every breath, a promise gleams,
In the heart of glacial dreams.

## Whispers in the Frigid Air

In the stillness, voices weave,
Secrets flutter, hard to believe.
Snowflakes drift like silent sighs,
Cold embraces beneath grey skies.

Frosty breaths upon the trees,
Nature's hush, a gentle tease.
Echoes linger, soft and rare,
Carried gently through the air.

Each step crunches on the ground,
Winter's pulse is all around.
Whispers rise with every chill,
Night unfolds with quiet thrill.

Frozen branches, crystal bright,
Glimmers dance beneath moonlight.
Time stands still in this embrace,
Frigid air, a soft, warm space.

Silent stories yet untold,
In the frost, the heart is bold.
Whispers echo, loud and clear,
Treasures found when winter's near.

# Dreaming Beneath the Ice

Beneath the surface, visions sway,
Frozen dreams in shades of grey.
Silent worlds where wishes flow,
Caught in time, with nowhere to grow.

Life is still, yet pulses deep,
In the freeze, our secrets keep.
Echoes brush against the cold,
Whispers of the tales retold.

Crisp reflections on the glass,
Memories that cannot pass.
In the depths, thoughts intertwine,
Drifting slow like aged wine.

Underneath this icy shell,
Dreams are safe and quiet dwell.
Hoping for a thawed embrace,
To bring warmth to this still place.

Resting quietly, time will show,
Life beneath, is set to grow.
Dreams await the light of spring,
When the thawed world starts to sing.

## **Frosted Mirrors**

Windows dressed in icy lace,
Nature's art, a fleeting grace.
Frosted mirrors tell our tales,
Whispers held in winter gales.

Glimmers trapped in every pane,
Reflections soft, yet not in vain.
Every shiver sparks a thought,
Frozen dreams that winter brought.

Patterns dance with every breath,
Life's embrace, a sweet duet.
Glistening hues of pale blue light,
In the stillness, hearts take flight.

The beauty of a fleeting chill,
Moments stay, yet time stands still.
Frosted mirrors hold our gaze,
Captured in this icy haze.

With every thaw, they melt away,
Stories lost at break of day.
Yet in the cold, we've felt the spark,
Frosted mirrors leave their mark.

## Chilled Echoes

In the frost, the whispers call,
Chilled echoes dance, then fall.
Silent paths through Nature's breath,
Capture life, come close to death.

Every step in icy air,
Carries dreams, light and fair.
Glistening trails of dreams once dreamed,
In the cold, our wishes gleamed.

Beneath the leafless boughs, we stand,
Feeling warmth from winter's hand.
Etched in ice, the stories blend,
Melodies in the clean, crisp end.

Echoes rise with every breeze,
Soft as snow on fallen leaves.
Nature hums a frosted tune,
Underneath the winter moon.

Chilled echoes linger in the night,
Hopes suspended, shining bright.
In this season's sweet embrace,
We find beauty in the place.

## Facets of Winter's Soul

Snowflakes dance in twilight's glow,
Whispers of the cold winds blow.
Underneath a silver sky,
Nature breathes a soft goodbye.

Frosted branches, quiet and still,
Chill of night, a gentle thrill.
The world wraps in a frozen sigh,
Heartbeats echo, time drifts by.

Crystals shimmer on barren ground,
In this stillness, peace is found.
Moonlight casts a serene spell,
Winter's soul, within us, dwells.

Through the pines, a lonesome call,
In the silence, shadows fall.
Every breath turns into steam,
Winter's heart, a fleeting dream.

Fires crackle, warmth embraced,
In the cold, love interlaced.
Together by the hearth we stay,
Winter's soul lights up the way.

## **Beyond the Crystal Veil**

Amidst the trees, a mystery lies,
Glistening shards under sky's sighs.
Each flake tells a story rare,
Beyond the crystal veil we dare.

As shadows shift with the twilight glow,
Whispers of magic softly flow.
Journey found in the winter's grace,
Hidden worlds we long to trace.

Glimmers dance in the heart of night,
Softly guiding with gentle light.
Through frozen paths, we wander far,
Seeking dreams where the night stars are.

Echoes of laughter fill the air,
Footprints in snow, memories shared.
Close your eyes, feel the embrace,
Beyond the crystal veil, we chase.

Time slows down in the silver glen,
Finding peace again and again.
Each moment fleeting, yet we remain,
In winter's arms, we feel no pain.

## Echoes in Frozen Silence

Beneath the hush of falling snow,
Whispers hide where cold winds blow.
Echoes dwell in a world so pure,
In frozen silence, hearts endure.

The world stands still, a paused embrace,
Magic woven through time and space.
Frigid air holds tales untold,
In winter's arms, we're fiercely bold.

Dancing shadows beneath the trees,
Softly carried on the breeze.
Notes of silence, a haunting song,
In frozen echoes, where we belong.

Frosted whispers reach the stars,
Tales of wonder, love and scars.
Every breath a cloud of white,
In the stillness, we find our light.

Memories linger like twilight's haze,
Lost in the warmth of winter's gaze.
Through the heart of the chilling night,
Echoes of love shine ever bright.

## Luminescent Frost


In the morning light, frost takes flight,
Glimmers dance with pure delight.
Nature's brush, a masterpiece,
In luminescent hues, we find peace.

Crystalline paths weave through the trees,
Each step crackles with winter's pleas.
Traces of magic underfoot,
In every flake, a silent root.

Sunrise breaks, the world aglow,
Transforming everything below.
A radiant blanket hugs the earth,
In luminescent frost, we see rebirth.

Each breath taken, a frosty mist,
Moments captured, too sweet to resist.
Wonders whisper through icy air,
In winter's grasp, we are aware.

Time seems lost in this icy dance,
Caught between a fleeting chance.
Underneath the dazzling sheen,
We find solace, pure and keen.

## Bound by the Chill

The wind whispers softly, a haunting song,
In the silence of winter, where shadows belong.
Frost clings to branches, a delicate lace,
Nature's own canvas, a tranquil embrace.

Every breath fogs up, a ghost in the air,
As footsteps leave imprints, a dance laid bare.
Beneath the cold surface, a warmth still resides,
In the heart of the frost, where magic abides.

Stars twinkle brightly, in the dark velvet sky,
Each sparkle a story, just waiting to fly.
The chill wraps around, a comforting shawl,
Binding the earth in a winter's thrall.

In this realm of ice, where time feels still,
Moments stretch eternally, a soft diurnal thrill.
A world transformed, in shades of white,
Bound by the chill, we embrace the night.

## **The Beauty of a Frozen Heart**

In the depths of winter, emotions run cold,
A heart like a glacier, where stories unfold.
Yet beneath the surface, warmth flickers bright,
A dance of the shadows, a spark in the night.

Silence envelops, where whispers are few,
In the beauty of frost, old wounds feel anew.
Icicles glisten, like tears turned to glass,
Reflecting the strength, in the trials that pass.

Snowflakes like wishes, fall soft from the sky,
Each one a promise, a reason to try.
The cold may be biting, but hearts can ignite,
In the beauty of frozen, we find our own light.

Embers lie hidden, beneath icy shells,
A story of struggle that each heart compels.
Through the chill, we journey, with courage, we fight,
Finding beauty in frozen, in love's pure insight.

## **Enchanted Snowflakes**

Dancing through the air, like dreams long deferred,
Snowflakes twirl gracefully, each whisper unheard.
Unique in their pattern, like stars in the night,
Enchanted and fleeting, a magical sight.

They blanket the earth in a shimmering white,
Transforming the world into pure delight.
Each flake is a whisper from winter's cool breath,
A reminder of beauty, in cycles of death.

With every soft landing, they cradle the ground,
Creating a world where silence is found.
They gather in clusters, on branches and stone,
An enchanted embrace, in a chill that's their own.

As dawn breaks the stillness, they catch the first light,
A symphony sparkling, awash with delight.
In the heart of the cold, they weave tales so grand,
Enchanted snowflakes, like magic, they stand.

## **Mirrors of the Frosted Night**

When darkness descends, and stars start to gleam,
The world is encased in a shimmering dream.
Frost paints the windows, with delicate art,
Mirrors reflecting the chill in my heart.

Each crystal is formed, a story retold,
Of glances exchanged in the bitter and bold.
The night wraps around, a blanket of fears,
Yet glimmering softly, like laughter through tears.

The moon casts its glow on the frost-kissed ground,
In the stillness of night, serenity's found.
These mirrors remind us of journeys we've known,
Reflecting our battles, how we've grown.

In shadows, they shimmer, revealing our past,
A testament to moments, both silent and vast.
The beauty of night is a story, a rite,
In mirrors of frost, our souls take to flight.

## Numbed Light

In the dawn's weak glow, shadows stretch wide,
Silence drapes gently as dreams collide.
Colors fade slowly, lost in the haze,
Hope flickers dimly through the sun's maze.

Chilled whispers curl like smoke from the past,
Time drips slowly, moments contrast.
Fading echoes linger in the air,
Quiet reminders, a muted prayer.

Beneath the surface, a pulse remains,
Yearning for warmth in the autumn rains.
A flicker of life in a world grown cold,
Memories scattered, stories untold.

As daylight wanes, stars begin to speak,
Illuminating paths for the brave and the weak.
Through the numbness, a flicker glows bright,
Guiding the heart through the depths of night.

**Distorted Shadows**

Beneath the streetlamp, shadows take flight,
Twisted shapes dance in the pale moonlight.
Whispers of secrets, lost in the breeze,
Echo through alleys, a haunting tease.

Figures from memories, faces undefined,
Drifting like ghosts in the corridors of mind.
Time stretches thin, like fabric worn,
Tracing the edges where hope is torn.

A flicker of laughter, a shadow of pain,
In the depths of darkness, there's much to gain.
Reflected in puddles, truths start to sway,
In the web of the past, we lose our way.

Yet in the chaos, light finds its place,
Illuminating corners with delicate grace.
Embrace the distortions, let the heart sing,
For shadows, too, carry the gifts they bring.

## Winter's Embrace

Under a quilt of shimmering white,
Silence descends with the fall of night.
Trees wear crystals like crowns of glass,
Whispers of winter in whispers that pass.

Frosted breath dances in the air,
Holding the warmth of memories rare.
Each flake that falls tells a tale anew,
In the hush of the world, there's magic too.

Footsteps crunch on the blanket below,
A melody played soft and slow.
Through the embrace of the winter's spell,
Hearts find a sanctuary where dreams dwell.

Night's velvet curtain wraps us tight,
Beneath the stars, everything feels right.
In the calm of this silent delight,
We find our solace, our own guiding light.

## Hushed Frost

In the stillness, frost begins to creep,
For the world lies silent, lost in deep sleep.
Nature's breath held in a crystalline sigh,
Under the glow of a starlit sky.

Each leaf adorned with a delicate gleam,
Whispers of winter, a muted dream.
The world slows down, time starts to freeze,
Wrapped in the beauty that brings us peace.

A gentle hush blankets the land,
Leading us softly, hand in hand.
In the frosted air, we shed our fears,
Finding warmth in the chill of the years.

Through the twilight, our hearts align,
In the embrace of the cold, we find.
A lullaby sung by the night's embrace,
Together we wander, lost in this space.

## The Cry of the Frigid Moon

In the night, a pale light glows,
Casting shadows, where the cold wind blows.
The world draped in a shivering hue,
Whispers secrets, old yet new.

Crystals form in the icy air,
Memory stirs, of warmth laid bare.
Stars above, like eyes that weep,
Guarding dreams while the world sleeps.

Frosted branches, trees stand tall,
A haunting silence, the night's soft call.
The moon, a sentinel in the dark,
Guides lost souls, igniting a spark.

Beneath her gaze, the earth lies still,
Time frozen, against nature's will.
In her glow, hearts are bound,
To the secrets of the frozen ground.

A melody soft, echoes within,
An ancient tale, where we begin.
The cry of the moon, a song so bright,
Illuminates the depths of night.

## **Frostbound Reflections**

A mirror lies on the frozen lake,
Reflecting dreams we dare to make.
Beneath the glass, the world does breathe,
Whispers of autumn, tangled in weave.

White clouds drift with gentle ease,
Curtains of snow flurry on a breeze.
Every flake, a story untold,
In frosty fingers, the past we hold.

Winding paths through the winter's chill,
Every step carries a silent thrill.
Footprints vanish with the light of day,
Yet shadows linger, unwilling to sway.

Across the fields, the silence reigns,
Nature's heart beats with the strains.
Frostbound dreams in the cold embrace,
A dance of time, a fleeting grace.

Reflections stir in the crystal night,
Echoes of warmth, a distant light.
In winter's grasp, we find our way,
Amidst the chill, our hopes will stay.

## Winter's Silent Portrait

Canvas of white, the world doth wear,
Traces of beauty, nowhere to spare.
Each corner holds a tranquil scene,
Nature's brush strikes, soft and serene.

Barren trees stand in quiet thought,
Stories of summer, gently caught.
A lingering chill in the breath of air,
Whispers of warmth, love laid bare.

Footsteps echo on the powdery ground,
In every silence, a yearning sound.
Nature's spell weaves a gentle plight,
In winter's arms, wrapped close and tight.

Soft snowfall blankets, a temporary rest,
Moments of peace, in a world so blessed.
Starry skies weave their dreams at night,
Winter's portrait, a wondrous sight.

With every flake that graces the earth,
Comes a reminder of joy's rebirth.
In the heart of cold, warmth ignites,
Bestowed by winter's tender nights.

## Glacial Echoes

Echoes of cold, through valleys wide,
Nature's rhythm, where shadows bide.
Each breath a mist, a haunting sound,
 Whispering tales that gather round.

Mountains rise, their peaks adorned,
With glistening ice, endlessly worn.
In the silence, the world takes flight,
 Carving paths within the night.

A wind gently kisses frosted pines,
Rustling stories from ancient lines.
The glaciers sigh, their secrets deep,
Guardians of time, in silence keep.

Cracks in the ice, a symphony's call,
 Rippling whispers across the fall.
 In the embrace of winter's hold,
 Stories of life and love unfold.

As daylight fades and shadows blend,
The glacial echoes, they never end.
In every chill, a warmth we find,
Connecting the heart, the body, the mind.

## **Reflections in Crystal**

Transparent whispers in the night,
Captured dreams in shard and light.
Glimmers dance on surfaces clear,
Fragmented visions, close and near.

Each angle sings a story's tune,
Echoes soft of the rising moon.
Moments frozen, memories hold,
A crystal world where tales unfold.

Beneath the surface, truths reside,
In every glint, emotions collide.
The beauty lies in fleeting glance,
Caught in the mirror's fragile dance.

Layers deep of joy and strife,
Reflecting the essence of life.
Shattered pieces, yet still whole,
In crystal's grasp, we find our soul.

In quiet corners, shadows play,
As light and darkness intertwine their way.
In every shard, a path to see,
A realm of wonder, endlessly free.

**Frosty Reveries**

Gentle breath of winter's grace,
Whispers softly in frozen space.
Snowflakes drift with silent glee,
Painting dreams on every tree.

Chill of air and frosted ground,
In every flake, a story found.
Nature's canvas, white and bright,
Shimmering soft in morning light.

Footsteps crunch on paths untold,
In quiet woods, the heart grows bold.
Frosted branches, a delicate lace,
Memories captured in winter's embrace.

Stars blink down from velvet skies,
Illuminating dreams that rise.
Through the cold, warmth starts to bloom,
As frosty reveries break the gloom.

In the hush, reflections seem,
Kindled by a glimmering dream.
Nature's pause, a moment's bliss,
In frosty realms, we find our kiss.

## Shivering Insights

Whispers flutter through the trees,
Secrets carried by the breeze.
In the chill of twilight's hour,
Nature's pulse, a gentle power.

Frozen thoughts in icy air,
The mind unwinds in tranquil glare.
Beneath the stars, we seek and find,
Shivering truths that free the mind.

Every breath, a frosted cloud,
Hope encased, yet fierce and proud.
In the silence, insights glow,
A journey started, paths to sow.

Embrace the cold, let feelings flow,
Among the shadows, visions grow.
In the stillness, a spark ignites,
Within the heart, shivering insights.

As winter wraps the earth in white,
Awakens dreams, ignites the light.
Through every chill, a warmth holds tight,
In shivering moments, we take flight.

# **Silent Resonance**

In the hush of lingering night,
Echoes dance in soft moonlight.
Silent whispers, shadows stretch,
Nature's heart, in calm, we fetch.

Every leaf a story tells,
In whispered tones where wonder dwells.
A symphony of silent grace,
In stillness found, our rightful place.

Rippling waters, tranquil flow,
Mirroring life in undertow.
Quiet depths hold ancient songs,
Resonance where the soul belongs.

Time stands still in solitude,
In gentle pauses, we are renewed.
Every heartbeat finds its chance,
In silent resonance, we advance.

Let the world fade, just for now,
In silence deep, we take a bow.
Through echoes soft, we pierce the veil,
In silent resonance, we set sail.

## Frozen Facets

Icicles hang from rooftops low,
Reflecting light in a crystal glow.
Each breath is a whisper, a fog in the air,
Nature's artistry, delicate and rare.

Snowflakes dance in a silent ballet,
Covering the earth in a soft white array.
Footprints trace paths in the powdery frost,
In the hush of winter, time seems lost.

Branches are draped in a powdered lace,
A divine transformation, a magical place.
Frozen droplets from branches fall down,
Nature wears her diamond crown.

Days short and the nights long,
A world transformed to a winter song.
Under the moonlight, shadows play,
In the heart of winter, peace holds sway.

As dusk settles in, a stillness reigns,
In the frozen facets, beauty remains.
Wrapped in a quilt of white and blue,
Winter's embrace, a world anew.

## A Mirror's Chill

Beneath the surface, reflections lie,
A mirror's chill under the darkened sky.
Windows of frost trace tales untold,
Capturing whispers from the bitter cold.

Each sheen of ice, a story unfolds,
Of the past, of memories, of dreams so bold.
In the quiet night, the world feels near,
Trapped in the glass, crystal clear.

The wind breathes softly, a ghostly sigh,
As shadows flicker and moments fly.
A dance in stillness, a breath held tight,
In the mirror's chill, day meets night.

Glistening surfaces reflect our fears,
Echoing laughter, the silence tears.
In every shimmer, a piece of the soul,
Fragments of life, the memories roll.

Underneath the moon, a tranquil glaze,
Chilled reflections in the winter's haze.
Where echoes linger, shadows blend,
In a mirror's chill, we ascend.

## Silence Between Snowflakes

In the quiet hush of falling snow,
A gentle peace begins to grow.
Each flake unique, a whispered grace,
Nature's breath in a serene embrace.

Silence blankets the world outside,
As winter's coat begins to glide.
Footsteps muffled on the frosty ground,
In the silence, a beauty profound.

Snowflakes twirl like dancers in flight,
Casting shadows in the pale moonlight.
The air crisp, inhaling the calm,
Wrapped in winter's soothing balm.

Between each flake, a moment held,
A stillness forming, a spell compelled.
In frozen whispers, the earth stands still,
Embracing the magic, the peaceful thrill.

As night descends on the snowy spree,
Silence lingers, a melody free.
Here in the stillness, dreams intertwine,
In the silence of snowflakes, hearts align.

## Shards of Winter

In the frosty dawn, the world awakes,
Shards of winter, the landscape breaks.
Sunlight glitters on fields of white,
A tapestry woven, warm and bright.

Crystals fracture, a prism's glow,
Sprinkling magic where cold winds blow.
Each shard a story, a frozen tear,
A glimpse of joy, a hint of fear.

Amidst the chill, a beauty thrives,
In the heart of winter, life survives.
Bare branches contrast against the sky,
A stark reminder of moments that fly.

The air is sharp, a breath of ice,
Echoing nature's precise device.
Night cloaks the day in a velvet sheen,
Where shadows dance and dreams convene.

As twilight drapes its silken veil,
The shards of winter weave their tale.
In the stillness, life finds its art,
With each icy shard, a beating heart.

## Ethereal Frost

A whisper in the morning light,
Crystal veins on branches tight,
Each breath a cloud, so soft and pale,
Nature's splendor, an icy veil.

Footsteps crunch on frozen ground,
In silence, beauty can be found,
A tranquil hush, the world seems still,
As frosted dreams the heart can fill.

The sun ascends, a gentle rise,
Unveiling hues beneath blue skies,
Glistening jewels on every leaf,
Moments wrapped in winter's grief.

Stars at dusk twinkle with grace,
As night wraps all in a cold embrace,
Frosted whispers dance in the air,
Ethereal magic everywhere.

And when the moon casts silver beams,
The world awakes from its frozen dreams,
Each flake a story, a soft release,
In winter's grasp, we find our peace.

## Winter's Quiet Dashboard

The car sits still, covered in snow,
A silent witness to winds that blow,
Windshield's frost like a painter's art,
In winter's quiet, stillness start.

Raindrops frozen on the glass,
Moments paused, as seconds pass,
A dashboard reflects fleeting light,
While shadows dance in the fading night.

The heater hums a soft, warm song,
A cocoon where the soul belongs,
Outside, the world in white attire,
Blankets crisp, with dreams to inspire.

Headlights pierce the chilling mist,
As snowflakes fall, one can't resist,
The beauty found in quiet rides,
In winter's arms, the heart confides.

And as we travel through the freeze,
Each journey brings a subtle ease,
A dashboard's comfort, a gentle sigh,
In this still moment, we learn to fly.

# Frost-Painted Visions

Windows dressed in frosty lace,
Nature's artwork, a fleeting grace,
Light refracts in prism hues,
Whispers of winter, soft like muse.

The landscape shimmers, crystalline bright,
Frost-kissed mornings, pure delight,
Each step reveals a story told,
Through icy paths, bold dreams unfold.

Clouds drift lazily, gray and light,
In this serene, tranquil sight,
Layers of frost on rooftops lie,
Underneath the wide, open sky.

A canvas fresh, where outlines wane,
In the chill, a quiet refrain,
Seasons whisper through the veil,
Frost-painted visions, rich and frail.

In twilight's glow, the world transforms,
As winter's eye in silence warms,
Each breath a frosted sigh of bliss,
In this moment, we find our kiss.

## Stillness in Chill

A calm descends, the world holds breath,
In nature's grasp, we dance with death,
Stillness lingers, the air so crisp,
In winter's clutch, we softly slip.

Trees stand bare, unique in grace,
A frozen dance, an icy pace,
Beneath the stars, our hearts ignite,
In stillness found, the world feels right.

Whispers of snowflakes drift and swirl,
Time slows down in this chilly whirl,
With every flake, a memory spun,
In moments shared, we become one.

Paths untraveled in shadows dip,
With every step, our spirits grip,
Finding warmth in the cold embrace,
In stillness held, we find our place.

So let us bask in winter's chill,
Embrace the silence, find the thrill,
Amidst the frost's enchanting spell,
In stillness, hear the heart's soft bell.

## Crystalline Whispers

In the hush of dawn's embrace,
Nature sings a hidden tune.
Each breath, a fragile echo,
Crystalline whispers under the moon.

Frozen leaves dance in the light,
Glistening like stars in flight.
Time slows in this serene space,
As if the world holds its breath tight.

Softly, the shadows play,
Sketching dreams along the way.
Gentle winds whisper secrets,
In a world where night turns to day.

Amidst the pines, the frost gleams,
Every branch, a silver dream.
Nature's art in quiet strokes,
As morning weaves its golden beams.

A tapestry of silence spun,
Where every moment feels like fun.
Lost in this crystalline wonder,
We linger until day is done.

## The Silence of Chilled Waters

Beneath the ice, the river waits,
With secrets deep, it contemplates.
Shimmering stillness cloaked in white,
A serene world that captivates.

Each ripple holds a whispered tale,
Of journeys long, of winds that sail.
In the arms of winter's grace,
The water's song becomes a veil.

Trees stand guard in hushed repose,
Enfolded in a glistening pose.
Nature's breath, a frosty kiss,
Encircles all where silence grows.

Footsteps crunching on the shore,
Tales of warmth and winter lore.
Chilled waters hold a timeless peace,
Whispering softly, evermore.

## Ethereal Frost

Frosted dreams adorn the night,
Casting crystals, pure and bright.
Each breath forms a fleeting cloud,
In this realm of soft twilight.

Moonlight gently hugs the snow,
Painting landscapes, soft and slow.
Stars blink through an icy veil,
As the world begins to glow.

Ethereal light fills the air,
Magic held in winter's stare.
Whispers linger in the chill,
Hope reborn with every prayer.

Every branch, a work of art,
Nature's canvas, purest part.
In the quiet, spirits dance,
As frost and wonder intertwine their heart.

Caught in time, this frosty spell,
A soothing wave where silence dwells.
In the stillness, we find peace,
In ethereal frost, all is well.

## Shadows on Frozen Stillness

In the grip of winter's breath,
Shadows linger, beckoning death.
Upon the lake's glassy face,
A ballet of dreams, held in stealth.

Silhouettes dance beneath the stars,
Whisper secrets from afar.
In this hushed, enchanted night,
Where frost lays bare the hidden scars.

Glistening branches touch the sky,
As the moon begins to sigh.
A world wrapped in frozen stillness,
In shadows where the echoes lie.

In twilight's grasp, a mystery,
Entwined with whispered history.
Each moment, taut and fragile,
In this space of reverie.

Awakened hearts find solace here,
In winter's cold embrace, so dear.
Where shadows paint their stories bold,
On frozen stillness, crystal clear.

## Beneath the Ice

Silent shadows lie below,
Where whispers dance in frozen flow.
Secrets held in frozen gaze,
Time suspended in icy haze.

Fractured light cascades like rain,
Colors flicker, soft, arcane.
Beneath the crust, a world unseen,
Nature's art in silence glean.

Ethereal echoes softly wail,
In this realm where dreams prevail.
Crystals weave a tale so bright,
Beneath the ice, a realm of light.

Cascading shadows, forms anew,
Tales of life and death in view.
Whispers murmur through the night,
Beneath the ice, the world feels right.

Here the past and future blend,
In the stillness, time won't end.
Nature's pulse beats soft and low,
Beneath the ice, the spirits glow.

## **Glacial Dreams**

In the stillness, visions rise,
Chasing echoes of the skies.
Glacial dreams in frosty breath,
Whispers dance near edges of death.

Mountains loom, their shadows cast,
Reflecting futures, tied to past.
In the chill, stories unfold,
Carved in ice, the heart is bold.

Winds of change, a gentle sigh,
Caress the dreams that float nearby.
Silent wishes, softly spun,
Glacial tales have just begun.

Frozen rivers bend and flow,
Carrying whispers from below.
In the quiet, hope still gleams,
Lost in glacial, fleeting dreams.

Stars above like jewels bright,
Bathing earth in silver light.
In this place, our spirits soar,
Seeking more, forevermore.

## **Echoes in Cold**

In the silence, secrets call,
Echoes linger, soft and small.
Whispers dance on frigid air,
Stories woven, threads laid bare.

Mountains echo ancient sighs,
Welcoming the winter skies.
Each breath shared, a fleeting bond,
In the cold, we wander fond.

Frosted winds, they sweep so wide,
Caught in dreams we cannot hide.
In the stillness, hearts will unfold,
Whispering secrets, echoes bold.

Through the night, the shadows creep,
In the cold, the thoughts run deep.
Navigating through the ice,
Finding warmth in sacrifice.

Time stands still, yet flows like stream,
In the echoes, we find dream.
Caught between the dark and light,
In cold silence, truth takes flight.

## Reflections of Frost

Morning glimmers, frost-kissed dawn,
Nature's beauty gently drawn.
Reflections dance on icy panes,
A fleeting glimpse as daylight wanes.

Each crystal captures moments near,
Woven memories linger here.
In the quiet, life displayed,
Frosty patterns, bright arrayed.

Glittering trees stand proud and tall,
Frozen whispers, nature's call.
In this realm, our spirits soar,
Reflections of what came before.

Softly falling flakes descend,
Blanketing earth, a soothing friend.
In the chill, warmth unfolds,
Stories of the heart retold.

As daylight fades, shadows creep,
In the frost, our dreams we keep.
Nature's wonder, pure and bright,
Reflections of frost, a tranquil sight.

## The Balance of Ice

In stillness rests the frozen lake,
A mirror made of crystal dreams.
Each flake a whisper, soft and sweet,
Holding stories, frozen beams.

Beneath the surface, depths conceal,
Moments trapped in icy grace.
The world above in silence feels,
A tranquil, cold, embracing space.

Time slips past like falling snow,
Layers hide the warmth we knew.
Each layer thick, yet fragile flow,
In every shard, a glimmer true.

The dance of light, a gentle play,
Reflects the beauty of the past.
A fleeting glimpse of yesterday,
In crystal arms, forever cast.

Yet warmth will come to kiss the frost,
To melt the ice and free the soul.
But in this moment, time is lost,
The balance struck, the heart is whole.

## **Crystalized Memories**

Fragmented visions, sharp and clear,
In glassy forms, they twist and turn.
Each memory a fleeting sphere,
With warmth of life, a fire to burn.

Fractured pieces of the heart,
Remnants of laughter, joy and tears.
Like shards of ice, they play their part,
In sculpting paths throughout the years.

In winter's clutch, the echoes fade,
Yet spark a light, a soft embrace.
Each moment held, a masquerade,
Woven deep within time's lace.

Crystalized, they shine so bright,
In shadows cast by fleeting days.
A tapestry of dark and light,
Each thread a tale that softly sways.

Let not these memories slip away,
For in their glow, we find our way.
A frozen heart of yesterday,
In crystal light, forever stay.

## Frozen in Time

Caught within the breath of frost,
Time stands still in icy grip.
A moment cherished, never lost,
Held tight within winter's sip.

The world outside moves fast, unkind,
But here, the chill preserves the grace.
Each snowflake falling, softly blind,
Paints a memory in its place.

Laughter echoes through the cold,
In frosty air, the warmth remains.
As stories of the young and old,
Are stitched in snow, like silver chains.

A whisper soft, in frosty breath,
Each beat of time encapsulates.
In frozen worlds, there's little death,
For moments live, and never abates.

So let us dream in winter's hold,
For here, the past can still unfold.
Within this realm of ice, behold,
The beauty in the frost, retold.

## **Iced Nostalgia**

Memories polished, cold and bright,
In pools of ice, reflections gleam.
Faded faces hold me tight,
In dreams that swirl like winter's dream.

The laughter echoes in the frost,
A dance within the silent streets.
Though seasons change, we feel the lost,
In every breath, nostalgia greets.

The world outside drifts on in haste,
While time, like snow, begins to lay.
Each whispered thought, a tender taste,
Of summers past, now far away.

Yet in this chill, we find the love,
A warmth that warms the frozen ground.
In fleeting moments high above,
We hold the past, forever bound.

So let the ice enfold our hearts,
Embracing years both sweet and shy.
In iced nostalgia, life imparts,
An everlasting, tender sigh.

## **Shimmering Refractions**

Light dances on the lake's face,
Colors blend in a gentle embrace.
Ripples whisper secrets untold,
Nature's canvas, a sight to behold.

Fragments of sun in every wave,
Reflecting the warmth that we crave.
Moments captured in fleeting time,
Each glance is a melody, each shimmer a rhyme.

Through branches, the light filters in,
Awakening shadows where dreams begin.
A tapestry woven with gold and blue,
In the heart of the forest, a world so true.

The horizon blurs with the rush of night,
As stars emerge, twinkling bright.
Merging with the depths, silence falls,
Echoing beauty as twilight calls.

In this stillness, I find my peace,
Where every worry and doubt can cease.
In shimmering refractions, I roam,
The essence of nature, my eternal home.

## Twilight on Thawed Waters

A canvas of hues in the dusk's embrace,
Reflections of dreams softly trace.
The chill fades slowly, day sighs,
As the sun bids farewell in colorful dyes.

Gentle ripples cradle the light,
Whispers of twilight, day turns to night.
The sky blushes with an amber glow,
While secrets of water begin to show.

Birds retreat to their hidden nests,
As shadows grow and daylight rests.
Murmurs of nature, soothing and near,
In this tranquil moment, all is clear.

The horizon glimmers, a haunting refrain,
As laughter of crickets fills the lane.
On thawed waters, the world feels vast,
Every fleeting moment, a memory cast.

I breathe in the calm, I breathe out the day,
In twilight's embrace, I long to stay.
Each ripple a story, each star a sigh,
Under the velvet night, together we fly.

**Encased in Serenity**

A glimmer of hope in the still of dawn,
Where silence rests and the world is reborn.
Wrapped in the arms of the gentle breeze,
I find a haven beneath ancient trees.

Mossy blankets cushion each step,
Nature's embrace where shadows are kept.
A stream sings softly a lullaby sweet,
In this moment, my heart feels complete.

The leaves whisper secrets, the flowers nod,
In every detail, I find a façade.
Life slows down in this sacred space,
As I gather strength, my fears to erase.

Clouds drift lazily across the blue,
Painting the sky with a vibrant hue.
Wrapped in tranquility, I pause and reflect,
In the beauty of nature, I'm always suspect.

Time loses meaning in the peace I find,
As whispers of nature enrich my mind.
Encased in serenity, I feel the call,
To cherish each moment, to embrace it all.

## **Subzero Silhouettes**

Frosted images in the silver light,
Nature frozen in a crystal sight.
Branches adorned with delicate lace,
Subzero silhouettes begin to grace.

Whispers of winter coat the trees,
A tranquil hush carried by the breeze.
In this stillness, the world holds its breath,
Beauty interwoven with the chill of death.

The moon paints shadows on the snow,
Where dreams wander and soft winds blow.
In every corner, a secret kept,
As the winter's magic, in silence, crept.

Crystals glimmer in a ghostly gleam,
Reflecting the quiet of a frozen dream.
Underneath the surface, life may pause,
But in this stillness, nature finds its cause.

With each frosty breath, I feel alive,
In the heart of winter, I learn to thrive.
Subzero silhouettes shape my view,
In the icy embrace, I feel renewed.

**Veils of Cold**

In the stillness, snowflakes fall,
Blanketing the world, a quiet call.
Each breath a whisper, crisp and bright,
Veils of cold wrap the fading light.

Trees stand silent, adorned in white,
Nature holds her breath, as day turns night.
Footsteps echo on the frozen ground,
In the veils of cold, peace is found.

Moonlight dances on icy streams,
Casting shadows on forgotten dreams.
The world is hushed, a gentle sigh,
Wrapped in quiet, we watch time fly.

Frosted branches, sparkling grace,
Winter's magic, a soft embrace.
Under the stars, a tranquil scene,
In the veils of cold, we find serene.

With every breath, the chill we feel,
Hearts warm within, this season's seal.
In the silence, we hear the truth,
Veils of cold cradle our youth.

## **Timeless Glimmer**

In the twilight, stars ignite,
Whispers echo, soft and bright.
Moments linger, time stands still,
In the timeless glimmer, hearts fulfill.

Silver dreams float on the breeze,
Carried gently through the trees.
Each heartbeat tells a story rare,
In the timeless glimmer, we are bare.

Reflections dance on quiet lakes,
In every ripple, a truth awakes.
Every glance, a spark divine,
In the timeless glimmer, souls entwine.

Golden hues brush the horizon,
Morning breaks, a new season.
Hope is born with every ray,
In the timeless glimmer, night turns day.

Through shadows deep, we find our way,
In the light, we choose to stay.
Each step a rhythm, fate's soft chime,
In the timeless glimmer, we are prime.

## Whispering Ice

Beneath the frost, the earth sleeps tight,
Whispering ice in the pale moonlight.
Nature's secrets, soft and low,
Through the silence, whispers flow.

A crackling sound, the world awakes,
Icebergs shift, the river shakes.
In the cold, a story we weave,
With every breath, we dare believe.

Cascading down from mountain peaks,
The icy tongue, a voice that speaks.
In shimmering layers, beauty lies,
Whispering ice beneath the skies.

Time slips by, unnoticed here,
In the stillness, we draw near.
Hearts unite in the starkest chill,
Whispering ice, a promise will.

In frosted veins, our spirits soar,
With every flicker, we explore.
In nature's heart, we find our place,
Whispering ice, a soft embrace.

## Shattered Silence

In the quiet, echoes remain,
Whispers lost, but not in vain.
Memories linger, sharp and clear,
In shattered silence, we draw near.

Voices carried on the wind,
Stories untold, yet to begin.
Fleeting moments, shadows dance,
In shattered silence, we take a chance.

Light breaks through the darkened veil,
Cracks of sound, a whispered tale.
In the fragments, we piece together,
In shattered silence, we find forever.

Time cannot mend what's torn apart,
But in silence, we heal the heart.
Every silence holds a song,
In shattered silence, we belong.

A symphony of what once was,
Quietly echoing, just because.
In the depths, our spirits rise,
In shattered silence, truth underlies.

Milton Keynes UK
Ingram Content Group UK Ltd.
UKHW010230111224
452348UK00011B/640